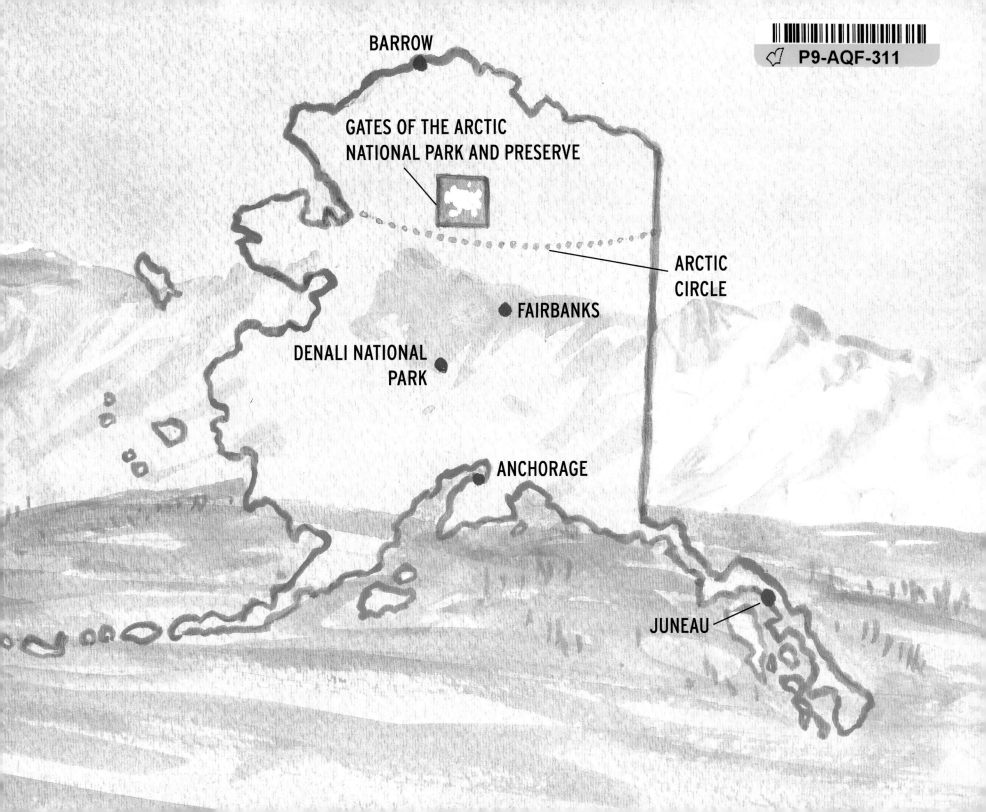

BARROW

GATES OF THE ARCTIC
NATIONAL PARK AND PRESERVE

ARCTIC
CIRCLE

FAIRBANKS

DENALI NATIONAL
PARK

ANCHORAGE

JUNEAU

For Pat Keogh, whose enthusiasm, love,
and appreciation of children's books is an inspiration —D. M.

To my beloved state of Alaska in hopes this book will bring a better
understanding of its wild natural wonders —J. V. Z.

First published in the United States of America in February 2010 by
Walker Publishing Company, Inc.
Visit Walker & Company's Web site at www.bloomsburykids.com

For information about permission to reproduce selections from this book, write to
Permissions, Walker & Company, 175 Fifth Avenue, New York, New York 10010

Library of Congress Cataloging-in-Publication Data
Miller, Debbie S.
Survival at 40 below / by Debbie S. Miller ; illustrated by Jon Van Zyle.
p.   cm.
ISBN: 978-0-8027-9815-2 (hardcover) • ISBN: 978-0-8027-9816-9 (reinforced)
1. Cold adaptation—Juvenile literature. 2. Zoology—Arctic regions—
Juvenile literature.
I. Van Zyle, Jon, ill. II. Title.
QH543.2.M55 2010   591.75'86—dc22   2009013328

Art created with acrylic on 300-lb coldpress watercolor paper
Typeset in Horley Old Style
Book design by Nicole Gastonguay

Printed in China by Printplus Limited, Shenzhen, Guangdong
(hardcover) 10 9 8 7 6 5 4 3 2 1
(reinforced) 10 9 8 7 6 5 4 3 2 1

All papers used by Walker & Company are natural, recyclable products
made from wood grown in well-managed forests. The manufacturing processes
conform to the environmental regulations of the country of origin.

ACKNOWLEDGMENTS

First, a huge thanks to Don and Tracie Pendergrast and Teri
McMillan for the opportunity to participate in the Gates
of the Arctic National Park's Artist in Residence program.
Exploring this beautiful, wild country and viewing the
wildlife offered the foundation for this book project.

Second, many thanks to all the wildlife biologists and
scientists who answered countless questions about animal
adaptations or who took the time to review and critique
my manuscript: David Klein, Brian Barnes, Trixie Lee,
Todd Sformo, Keith Echelmeyer, Susan Sharbaugh, Layne
Adams, John Burch, Jennifer Nielsen, Nancy Sisinyak,
Sverre Pedersen, Andres Lopez, Bill Hauer, Jan Rowell, Pat
Reynolds, Fran Mauer, Jim Lawler, Donna DiFolco, Richard
Shideler, Erich Follmann, Herb Melchior, and Kenelm
Phillip. Without the research and insights of these people, I
would not be able to adequately describe the fascinating lives
of these animals. Last, thanks to Richard Nelson for sharing
his wonderful animal recordings so that children can listen to
the world of the Arctic.

SURVIVAL AT 40 BELOW

Debbie S. Miller

illustrations by **Jon Van Zyle**

Walker & Company
New York

Along the Koyukuk River, towering mountains guard the magnificent valley. Their sheer faces watch the seasons change.

Click . . . click . . . click. Snapping hooves and grumbling voices fill the autumn air. With heads held high, a herd of caribou follows the river through Gates of the Arctic National Park.

These regal deer wear new coats of dense fur, with velvet antlers curving toward the sky. Ready for winter, the caribou have gained a thick layer of fat from summer grazing on the tundra.

Other arctic animals scurry and prepare for the coming eight months of snow. Chickadees and gray jays cache seeds and morsels of carrion, hiding the food in cracks beneath tree bark. Red squirrels pluck spruce cones and hurl them to the ground. They will tear open the cones and eat the spruce seeds through the winter. A weasel snatches a brown lemming and carries it to an underground food cache.

Nights grow colder. A thin layer of ice creeps across a pond near the river. Snug in their lodge, beavers rest after cutting many saplings for their underwater cache. Near their food pile, an Alaska blackfish paddles slowly through pond vegetation, searching for insect larvae. This bottom dweller can survive the winter in shallow frozen ponds with little oxygen. Along with gills, the blackfish has an unusual esophagus that can work like a lung, absorbing oxygen from the air. During the winter, this fish will find holes in the ice and breathe through its mouth.

Leaves rustle softly as a wood frog burrows into the duff of the forest floor. Suddenly, the frog feels its skin freezing. Its heart begins to beat rapidly. The frog's liver quickly produces lots of glucose. This sugary fluid, which the frog pumps through its body for several hours, will protect the insides of the cells from ice crystals. When more than three-quarters of its body freezes, the frog stops breathing and its heart stops beating.

But, like magic, the frog is still alive. Beneath the
insulating layers of duff and snow, this frozen amphibian
will hibernate until spring. It's a live frogsicle!

Farther up the valley, a small golden mammal is plump after a summer diet of tundra plants and seeds. As days grow shorter, the male arctic ground squirrel tunnels into the earth to prepare its burrow. He digs an underground chamber, about the size of a basketball, and stuffs it with grasses and tufts of caribou fur. Then he collects and stores seeds and berries.

Sik . . . sik . . . sik. The squirrel chatters a warning signal. Across the river, a grizzly bear browses on berries and digs up thick potato-like roots with her sharp claws. Alarmed by this huge predator, the squirrel dashes beneath the tundra. Like the squirrel, this grizzly will soon dig her winter den on a mountain slope.

As snowflakes swirl, the squirrel is ready to hibernate. He curls into a ball in his burrow, then slowly supercools his body, lowering his temperature to just below the freezing point of water. His heart rate gradually drops to three beats per minute, and his brain activity ceases. This ice-cold furry squirrel looks dead, but, amazingly, he is only in the inactive state of torpor.

After three weeks, something triggers the squirrel to wake up. His heart rate increases. He warms his body by burning brown fat. This insulating fat protects his vital organs and acts like a heating pad. Within several hours, his heartbeat and temperature are normal.

After rearranging his nest, the squirrel curls back into a ball and falls asleep. He dreams and sleeps soundly for about twelve hours. Then his body supercools again. Like a yo-yo, the squirrel warms himself, sleeps, and supercools about a dozen times during the winter to conserve enough energy to survive.

Above the squirrel's burrow, an arctic fox searches for prey.
The fox picks up the scent of voles beneath the snow. These
mouselike animals are huddling in their nest to keep warm.
Like an acrobat, the fox springs high into the air and pounces on
the voles. Breaking through the snow, he traps one by surprise.

The arctic fox keeps warm in frigid temperatures because he wears two winter coats. His dense underfur insulates him like the down in a fluffy sleeping bag. His thick outer coat has tiny air pockets inside the hair shafts, instead of color pigment. The snow-white coat perfectly camouflages the fox for hunting prey and escaping predators. Fur also covers the soles of his paws, and his big, bushy tail provides extra warmth.

Inch by inch, the layer of snow deepens with each winter storm. On a frigid January day, the temperature plummets to 40 below zero. Thick pond ice cracks and makes eerie sounds. The fluffy quilt of snow insulates and protects the many animals, plants, and insects beneath it. It is much warmer under the snow layer than in the open air.

Other animals are well adapted to survive the colder air temperatures above the ice and snow. Snowshoe hares and ptarmigan zigzag between the willow bushes. Both animals can travel lightly across the snow with insulated feet that help spread out their weight. But the ptarmigan can't survive the lethal night temperatures and fly off at dusk to seek shelter.

Puff! They dive into a drift of powdery snow. Invisible to the world, the ptarmigan roost inside their snow burrows, protected from predators and the extreme cold.

Another bird combats the deep freeze. A black-capped chickadee flits from tree to tree, eating his cached food. He must gain enough fat each day to survive the night.

But this small bird needs more than food to survive. He fluffs up his dense feathers for better insulation. Tiny muscles control the angle of each feather, while other muscles shiver to produce heat. The chickadee can also lower his temperature and metabolism to save energy. He roosts in a thick forest or in tree cavities that give him the best shelter.

While birds roost beneath a full moon, all is not quiet. A wolf howls on a distant ridge as caribou crunch through the snow with their broad hooves. These deer are well insulated for the Arctic by dense fur and hollow guard hairs. They sniff the snow and detect the smell of ashes from an old forest fire. Turning away, the caribou avoid this burned area.

Muzzles to the ground, the caribou later detect the mushroomlike scent of lichens. They dig craters and forage on clumps of these rootless plants. Their hooves and thin legs are well adapted for digging. A special liquid fat protects their joints. Blood traveling directly to the hooves helps warm the returning blood to the heart. This circular flow protects the legs and reduces heat loss.

While caribou wander, the grizzly bear is snug in her den with two newborn cubs. The drowsy bear nurses them and rests to save energy. The three survive off her large storehouse of fat. As she sleepily feeds her fast-growing cubs, she doesn't notice the faint sound of steps across the snow.

Sure-footed and agile, Dall sheep pick their way across the mountain slope. Fierce winds have blown snow off the alpine tundra, exposing frozen grasses and sedges. The sheep graze on these withered plants, then seek shelter from the wind by bedding down in the lee of some rocky crags.

Month by month, winter passes slowly. Backs to the wind, a group of musk oxen stands on the snow-covered tundra, conserving energy. Short legs, small ears, and fluffy underwool, known as *qiviut*, insulate musk oxen from even the deepest cold. As a newborn calf suckles milk from its mother, one musk ox sees wolves approaching and senses danger. Immediately, the musk oxen gather together. Shoulder to shoulder they form a circular wall of thick fur and horns. As one wolf draws near, a large bull lowers his deadly sharp horns. With a sudden burst, he charges the wolf.

Wheeling away, the wolf quickly retreats. The musk oxen continue to work as a team, charging and driving off the hungry wolves.

Trickle . . . tinkle . . . drip. The snow and ice begin to melt. As temperatures rise, bumblebees, butterflies, and other dormant insects begin to stir. A woolly bear caterpillar basks in the sun after being snow-covered for eight months. His dark, furry body traps the sun's heat. Inching his way to a budding willow, he chews on a tiny leaf.

These fuzzy creatures, and other northern insects, have antifreeze substances that prevent ice crystals from forming in their bodies. The woolly bear will spend up to fourteen winters in the Arctic as a caterpillar. Then this amazing survivor will transform into a moth, but for only one short summer!

One by one, moist leaves rustle near the pond. The wood frog slowly thaws out, and its heart beats once again. *rrrrRuk...rrrrRuk*. The frog begins calling for a mate, making a ducklike sound near the pond's edge. Slapping their tails in the open water, the beavers dive while the blackfish dart after prey on the pond's bottom. Farther up the valley, the male ground squirrel eats his stored cache of food, then leaves his burrow in search of a mate.

Hour by hour, day by day, the pulse of life increases with warmer June days and greening plants. Caribou feast upon a summer buffet, while playful grizzly bear cubs tussle and explore the tundra as their mother searches for prey. Birds that migrated south for the winter return to their birthplace, building nests on the tundra and filling the air with music. For more than two months the days will be endless, as the top of the world tilts toward the sun and the magical Land of the Midnight Sun explodes with life.

AUTHOR'S NOTE

I recently hiked through Gates of the Arctic National Park. My seventy-five-mile backpacking trip through the Brooks Range inspired me to write this book.

Each featured animal is well designed to live year-round above the Arctic Circle. I marvel at the unusual adaptations and survival strategies that allow these animals to live in one of the harshest environments on the planet. From frozen frogs and hibernating ground squirrels to active winter residents such as the wandering caribou and musk ox, the Arctic is home to an incredible diversity of life. It is my hope that this book gives readers a glimpse into the lives of these amazing creatures so that we can better understand, appreciate, and protect them.

Annie Caulfield

Today, animals of the Arctic face new challenges related to global warming and climate changes. Warmer and drier summers have caused larger and more frequent forest fires. Although the fires have destroyed many lichens, other green plants and shrubs have emerged from the carbon-rich soils. Some trees and shrubs are spreading farther north. Glaciers are melting more rapidly, and rivers are pouring more freshwater into the Arctic Ocean. The sea ice continues to melt, posing great risks to threatened polar bears and other animals that depend on ice habitats. What will be the effect of a warming climate on all these animals that are so well adapted to the Arctic? Scientists continue to study polar regions to monitor the dramatic changes and to look for long-term solutions to reduce greenhouse gas emissions.

GLOSSARY

Antifreeze: a substance that some insects produce in their tissues to avoid freezing; antifreeze lowers the freezing point of water and can block the formation of ice crystals within the insect's body tissues

Cache: a secure place to hide and store food

Carrion: the flesh of a dead animal

Duff: the leaves and dead plants that slowly decay on the forest floor; the duff and snow provide winter insulation for wood frogs, insects, and other animals

Fluff up: a term that refers to the fluffing of feathers or hairs to increase insulation; this fluffing, also known as *piloerection*, creates small air pockets and helps trap body warmth

Hibernation: an inactive, or resting, time of an animal during the winter; arctic animals hibernate to conserve energy and to survive the long winter, when food supplies are limited

Huddling: a winter strategy to reduce heat loss; animals, such as voles and beavers, huddle, or lie close together, in their communal nests to keep warm during winter

Insulation: anything, such as thick fur and feathers or a blanket of snow or duff, that helps to protect animals from cold temperatures

Lichens: the mossy rootless plants covering much of Alaska's tundra that are a marriage of two different primitive plants: algae and fungi; caribou depend on the slow-growing lichens as their most important winter food

Metabolism: the process by which all animals balance their intake of energy through food consumption with the use of that energy to maintain their body temperature, growth, and rate of activity

Qiviut: an Inupiaq word that refers to the fine and fluffy underwool of the musk oxen; qiviut is extremely dense and soft and among the warmest animal furs in the world

Shivering: producing body heat through involuntary muscle contractions; birds, such as the chickadee, shiver at times to help maintain the right body temperature

Torpor: an inactive, or dormant, state during hibernation when an animal's heart rate and body temperature are greatly reduced to conserve energy.

⤙ Record High and Low Temperatures ⤚

Arctic temperatures have grown warmer over the past century due to climate change and global warming. Yet animals still face extreme cold temperatures during Alaska's long winters. This chart shows the record high and low temperatures for Bettles, Alaska, near Gates of the Arctic National Park.

	Jan	Feb	Mar	Apr	May	Jun	Jul	Aug	Sep	Oct	Nov	Dec
°F	42	40	49	63	86	92	93	88	79	57	45	38
°C	6	4	10	17	30	33	34	31	26	14	7	3
°F	−70	−64	−56	−37	−10	27	29	22	0	−35	−57	−59
°C	−57	−53	−49	−38	−23	−3	−2	−6	−18	−37	−49	−51

Further Sources for Reading and Surfing

To learn more about Gates of the Arctic, America's northernmost national park, visit www.nps.gov/gaar.

To review photos and the student handbook about Gates of the Arctic, visit www.nps.gov/gaar/forkids/index.htm.

To take a virtual journey to this amazing park, watch the one-hour DVD *Gates of the Arctic: Alaska's Brooks Range*, by North Slope Productions (2008), available through www.alaskageographic.org/store/products/dvd-gates-of-the-arctic.

——————————————————— Read More About Alaska ———————————————————

Cobb, Vicki, and Barbara Lavallee. *This Place Is Cold*. New York: Walker & Company, 1990.

Crane, Carol, and Michael Glenn Monroe. *L Is for the Last Frontier*. Chelsea, MI: Sleeping Bear Press, 2002.

Miller, Debbie S., and Jon Van Zyle. *Arctic Lights, Arctic Nights*. New York: Walker & Company, 2003.

———. *Big Alaska: Journey Across America's Most Amazing State*. New York: Walker & Company, 2006.

———. *A Caribou Journey*. New York: Little Brown, 2000.

———. *A Polar Bear Journey*. New York: Walker & Company, 2005.

To hear the voices of the arctic animals in *Survival at 40 Below* and to learn more about the arctic region, visit the author's Web site at www.debbiemilleralaska.com.

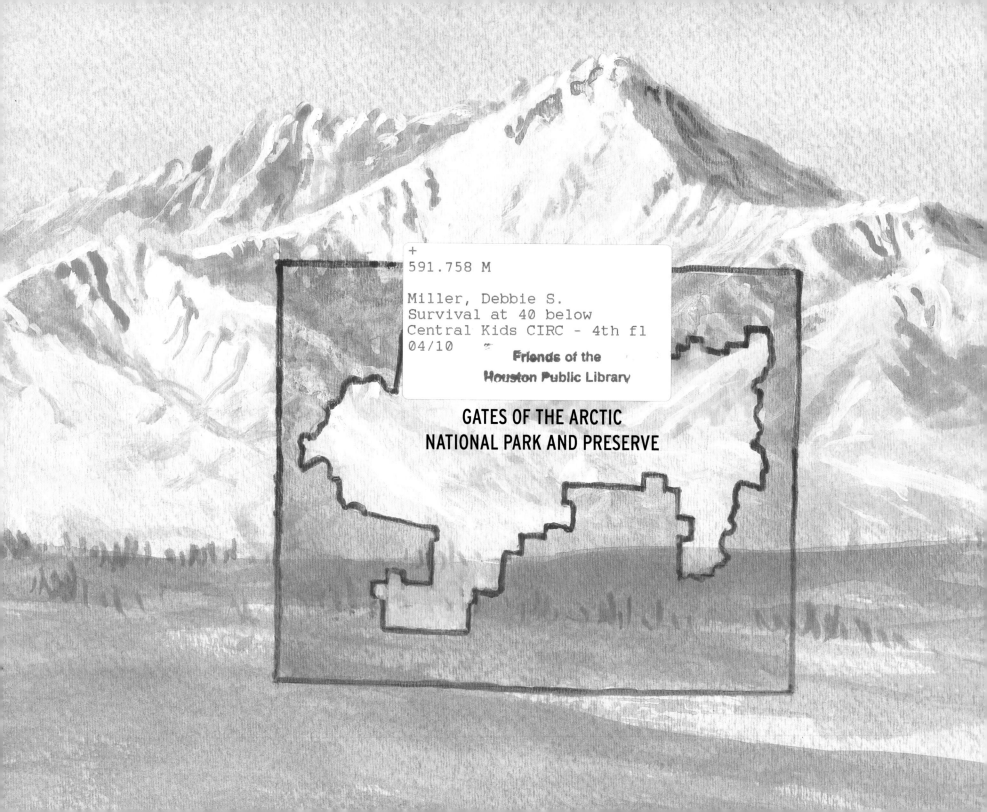

GATES OF THE ARCTIC
NATIONAL PARK AND PRESERVE

DATE DUE

MAY 2 1 1996		
APR 1 - 1998		
Grindley		
SEP 2 4 1998		
NOV 2 3 1998		
OCT 2 7 1999		
FEB 9 2000		
APR 2 0 2000		
MAY 3 0 2001 *Claudia Kkg*		
OCT 3 0 2001 *Kayla*		
JAN 1 6 2002 *May #2 ①*		
NOV 2 1 2002 *Esteban Kkg*		
Hays		

A
SPARK
IN THE
DARK

DEDICATION

To Connie and her remarkable strength of spirit,
And to the spark in each of us.

Copyright 1994 by Richard Tichnor and Jenny Smith

ISBN paperback 1-883220-26-2
hardcover 1-883220-25-4

Published by DAWN Publications
14618 Tyler Foote Road
Nevada City, CA 95959
(916) 292-3482

Printed on recycled paper using soy based ink
Printed in Hong Kong

10 9 8 7 6 5 4 3 2 1
First Edition

Designed by LeeAnn Brook
Type style is Papyrus

A SPARK IN THE DARK

WRITTEN AND ILLUSTRATED BY
RICHARD TICHNOR AND JENNY SMITH

DAWN Publications

Authors' Note

Stories of creation have been told by people everywhere, throughout time. These stories are not only fanciful tales from the past but are also allegories for the present. They are told symbolically so that each person can interpret the meaning in their own way. For example, the star in our story may represent God to some people, or to others, it may symbolize the explosion out of which our universe grew. On a more personal level, the star may symbolize any act of creation, a new burst of growth, or the creative spark within us. There are as many possible interpretations as there are readers.

The details of each creation story are different, reflecting the people who tell it. But if you listen carefully, you will find that all of these stories have similar underlying themes which tell us about ourselves—our place in the universe, our relationship with others, and our inner experience. That these stories are told by people all over the world shows us that inside we are not so different after all.

Through our story about creation we hope to remind people of what we all know but tend to forget in our everyday lives: that we all come from something larger than ourselves, and that we are all related in this way. Our story is also intended to remind people that we are all special, that each of us has the potential to bring light into the world.

This is the story
of a Star in the sky,
of where we all come from
and the answer to "why?"

It's about a blue ball,

a mountain and tree,

a light in our hearts,

and our reason to be.

A long time ago,

when the sky was

still dark...

In a faraway corner

flashed a bright little spark.

It grew into a Star,

way up in the sky.

Since no one was there,

no one asked "why?"

The Star loved the darkness,
it helped it to shine,
but was all by itself for a very long time.

And the Star grew lonely up there in the night,
with nothing to shine on or receive its star light.

So it made
a blue ball,
and spun it
around.
It was pretty
to look at,
but way
too
far
down.

So the Star made a mountain

grow up from the sea,

and said to itself,

"Now it's nearer to me."

But the mountain just sat there,

did nothing at all.

So it put a
green tree
on the
little blue ball.

Now the Star had the water,

the mountain and tree,

but still was not happy —

how could that be?

As the Star looked around and pondered its plight,

it spied down below its reflections of light —

Down on the water they danced and they swam.

The Star had an idea! The Star had a plan...

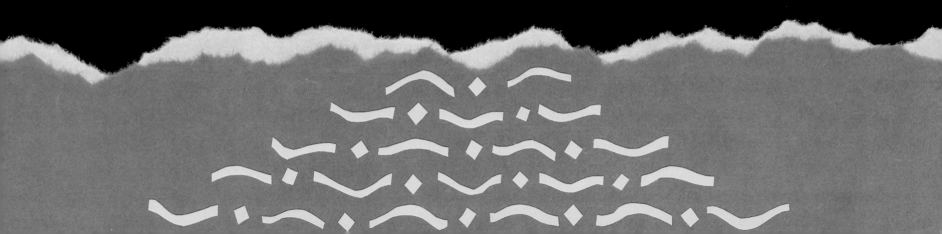

It took a deep breath,

'til it started to strain,

then starbeams fell down

on the mountain, like rain.

They burst into Beings of bright colored light. They could feel, they could hear, they could see every sight!

They ran, they skipped, they tumbled and played on the mountain and tree that the Star had just made.

And the Star was so happy with what it had done,
it fell asleep in the sky, tired out from the fun.

When day turned to night,
the Star opened its eyes,
to twinkling lights
that filled up the skies.

What happens,

you see...

in each child's heart

glows a piece of the Star,

of which we're all part.

In the sky up above, as each child dreams —

like the water, the darkness reflects their light beams.

While the children all sleep on the blue ball below,
their lights twinkle above in a beautiful glow.

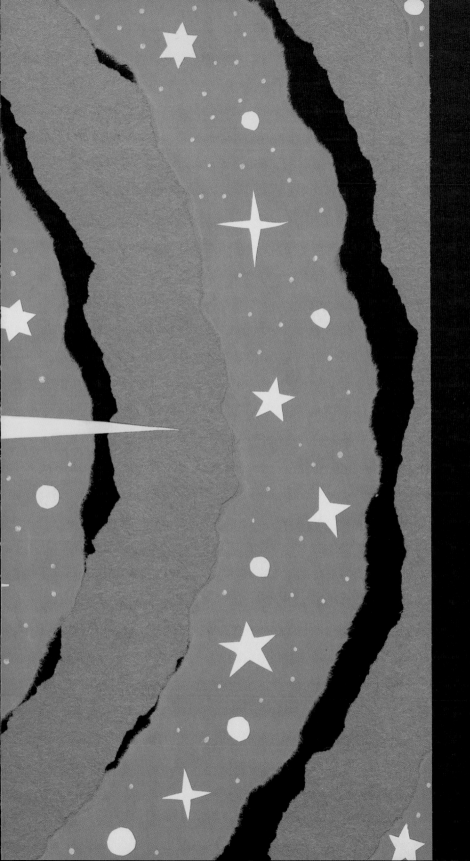

The star was delighted,
it sparkled with glee,
surrounded by lights
from within You and Me.

So remember, tonight
as you sleep in your bed,
a light from within
shines over your head.

And that is the story
of a world that began,
with all little children
as part of the plan.

No matter the color,

the shape big or small,

the Star loved them all

on the little blue ball.

ABOUT THE AUTHORS

A Spark in the Dark was written by Richard and Jenny as a Christmas gift for family members. The story was shaped by their shared interests and experiences. The mythological and symbolic elements were inspired by the writings of Joseph Campbell.

Richard began drawing and painting as a child; he is now an architect. Jenny has a master's degree in consciousness studies and has worked with both children and adults. Together they have shared many adventures: they've lived on Cape Cod; in France; and in a log cabin in the Sierra Nevada Mountains. They currently live at Lake Tahoe in California. *A Spark in the Dark* is their first book.

ACKNOWLEDGMENTS

We would like to thank our family and friends for their encouragement and interest. We also appreciate the support and efforts of everyone at Dawn Publications. And a special thanks to Bob, Glenn, and LeeAnn for their openness and guidance throughout the evolution of this book.

Dawn Publications is dedicated to helping people experience a sense of unity and harmony with all life. Each of our products encourages a deeper sensitivity and appreciation for the natural world. For a catalog listing our complete product line, please call (800) 545-7475.